By Yasanne Garrett

FORTIFIED FAITH PUBLICATIONS

Printed in the United States of America

First Edition, 2020

ISBN 978-1-7338619-1-5

Fortified Faith Publications
20 N. 78th St.
Belleville, IL 62223

Book formatted and edited by Fortified Faith Publication. Cover design by Jerry Garrett © 2020. All rights reserved.

Yasanne Garrett

I want to first thank my Lord and Savior Jesus Christ, my Granny, my parents, my kids: Curtis Jr, Michael, and Trinity; my God daughter Diamond, her daughter Chyna, many teachers and professors, many close friends, and all the people going into a storm, through a storm, or out of a storm.

A very special thanks to Dr. Jenny Mueller, academic advisor and my professor at McKendree University, who said "You are a poet", and Tamara Anderson for your professionalism, support, and encouragement. Thank you all so much!

Yasanne Garrett

Table of Contents

Yasanne Garrett

Yasanne Garrett

Admission of guilt fills the
Vibrant air of pink clouds of
Dust

Words clash the ears of judges to
Reach an agreement of satisfaction

Life sentence isn't enough
You're left picking up the
Pieces of detached hearts and families
As you search for
Normalcy in a crowded
Room of abusers and onlookers

I will be a child forever
I can't grow up in my mind
My age is an adult
My life is paralyzed in its youth

Pink ribbons fill my
Dreams with unraveled bows
Twirling through a vortex of reality and illusion.

The Storm Is Over Now

The Happening

Yasanne Garrett

There's a certain thing that happens...

A smothering of sorts,

A squeeze, gasping for air,

Longing for the wind to blow a touch that life isn't over

It has merely paused, searching for the meter to dance in the

light.

To feel, to heal, to believe that pain and loneliness ends with

me.

I must reverse this darkness.

That place that speaks in silent night whispering for me to go.

I listen and cry.

Where are the elders to tell me I can stand, lead, grow?

I wait. No one comes.

No deliverance, just deaf ears believing in nothing.

I must wait for me to catch up to embrace that little girl who

hides behind my cranium.

I must wait til I say hurt no more.

My darkest hour has passed.

The tingle has begun.

The Storm Is Over Now

Yasanne Garrett

Don't like my skin
Don't like within
Don't like the gains
Don't like the pain

I hate my voice
I hate this choice
I hate the war
I hate the chore

I dislike the tone
I dislike the wrong
I dislike the chase
I dislike the waste

I detest the green
I detest the mean
I detest this pull
I detest these rules

I abhor being alone
I abhor going along
I abhor this touch
I abhor you so much

I don't hate anymore
My heart has been restored
Even though you tried to break me
I am happy that I released me

I no longer hold me hostage
For sexual abuse and rape
God is bigger than my issues
He's better than good He's great

I unwind to a place of me
In the midst of the clarity
That I am absolutely 100 percent
Finally, in love with me.

The Storm Is Over Now

Me Too

Yasanne Garrett

It's not easy to acknowledge
The constant storm
Or admit that you're not
The norm

Day in, day out
Searching for truth
That is inside all of us
And have something to lose

To openly admit
This kind of abuse
Which way do I go
Which road do I choose

I'm lost. A street of
No ends drive
But it's time I stand up
And plunge in this dive

To fight the wicked hands
That old octopus
Who was a busy soul
Waiting to devour a young goose

All her goals
She should've achieved
But you were there
Being sneaky

So here I am
and I will be fine
Taking this storm
One abuser at a time

The Storm Is Over Now

The

Yasanne Garrett

Every day we meet
My old and new me
The me that suppressed
And the me that was free

That 1st me took all the pain,
The names, the abuse
The other me protected others
And my soul they did use

The 2nd me
The one I can't stand
To smooth it all out
She uses either & and

Doesn't want to acknowledge
That she's not okay
Sits in a room
And cries half the day

One day they will merge
The 1st and 2nd me's
Live as one instead
Of separately

Sip and Stir

Yasanne Garrett

Hot words poured off the lips
Of luscious love
They punched like glistening diamonds
In the purple pouch.

I wasn't ready to hear
About your indiscretions
The eardrums burned of truths
I ignored for years

It hurt. No lie.
It scoured my blotched heart
And beat unrhythmically
In every direction

With hand on the metal kettle
And one on the cracked mug
I emptily poured onto the loose tea leaves
and tears ran like salty streams

I stood tall to taste the elixir of
The past and realized I am free from
You and free to myself

The Storm Is Over Now

Yasanne Garrett

I dreamt I went for a swim
    My feet merged as 1
        And cheeks were puffed with air

I have a fear of water
    But today I am an expert

The water blue with oceanic wonder
    The urchins prick my scaly legs as I
        Lurk through the murky view

My eyes withstand the ebb and flow
    Of the strong hold currents
        I haven't come up for air
    No need
            As my lungs morph into steel cases
                Of gas exchanges

I move among the reefs and
    Tangled seaweed
        And taste a big gulp of crude and cruel oil

I cough and spit
    Realizing that I too have polluted such
        Beauty

The Storm Is Over Now

Me

Yasanne Garrett

I've come to the realization that
I'm not going to be anything more
Than what I am now.

I'm stuck in a world of
Physical emotional pain.
There's no door of opportunity just
Information trapped in my mind.

I see my children's fathers flourish
And the products of my DNA
Excel as I fall down.

I've been dealing with unbelievable sadness
That turns cold every January since the year of my rape.

Nobody can help Me but God.
I have no life.
Just words that make Me educated,
And a heart that makes Me kind,
And a spirit that makes Me
Feel what others can't.

My legacy is that there is no legacy.
2 crowns, and I still can't see the
Beauty in Me.

The mistreatments I've endured
Have strengthened Me
And hindered Me.

Love isn't for Me,
But I have been there before.

If I shared with you
My nightmares,
You will never
Fall asleep.

The Storm Is Over Now

Yasanne Garrett

Someone please come take away the pain

From me,

Though I thought I would just only cry

And then I see more reasons why

I see the old me.

She's gone she's broken

No dreams to tokens

Of love

No smiles no laughter

No forever after

Above....

Die please die the old me

Needs to leave

Die please die the new me

Is waiting to be unleashed

The Storm Is Over Now

Leg

Yasanne Garrett

The leg I stand on may not be strong.

It wavers on solid soil

It kicks the troubled rocks on my trail

It raises over elongated lumps in my path

It aches at the 1st sign of coldness

And locks up when red cells destruct.

The leg I stand on may not look attractive, but

My leg is the reason I am

Up

The Storm Is Over Now

From the time love pushed you into the world,

I became alive.

The softness of your breath and battered skin

Makes me shield you from the wiles of this earth.

Unnamed and small, I hold you against the staccato beats of my heart

As you rest your head upon the breast that birth you forward.

I'm forever indebted to you and your well-being.

Your continued growth will depend on my mental presence and

All of physicality of my being to mold you into the entity that God has in store for you.

You awake me.

They break me,

But we make the best of this union.

The Storm Is Over Now

My
Girl

Yasanne Garrett

Girl, where are you going and knowing?

Who told you to go afar and catch a star?

Who tole you to venture off and walk ahead of others?

Who told you to think for yourself?

Who told you to want more? Do more? Be more?

Who whispered in your ear to tell you that you can have it all?

What voice dared you to become you?

Look out the window

Fast brown trees go by

Air wipes your hair as

The train carries you to a new world

Awaiting your story.

Girl, you are independent.

Blazers of pins

Take it all in

Your world is yours to discover.

Enjoy this train ride!

The Storm Is Over Now

Yasanne Garrett

The one who cares
The one who shares
The one who disappears around those who are here.
The one who knows
The one who grows
The one who's not afraid to face the unknown.
The one who's in charge
The one who acts hard
The one who gets used when letting down her guard.
The one who is single
The one who doesn't mingle
The one who forgives those without letting it linger.
The one who's last
The one who carries the past
I'm the sister that's built to last.

The Female Silhouette

Yasanne Garrett

Traces of me doesn't start with
The linear outline of my curves.
It encompasses the shape of my
Inner core, knowledge, skills
Tongues, devotion to God and my family.

My mind stores past hurts and joys
Present promotions and
Arrangements of textures, perms, naturals, and braids.

My lips have spoken words of evil
To my sister and brothers,
To the world,
To the angst at glass ceilings
Harkened the undateables not ready for a strong
Woman draped in leadership.
My heart beats rhythmically to the
Gamut of men who didn't love me but
I loved expansively.

My legs hurt from the
Disappointed employment to climb
My way to the level of
Underappreciation, deception, disloyalty
Of all people.

My feet solidified
By walking miles in
The ancestral shoes of
My great great granny and those I never knew.

The Storm Is Over Now

The shape of us is
Dramatic, yet subtle
Muted, yet loud
Pragmatic, yet creative.

Created shapely to be the carriers
Of pain and chains.

Yasanne Garrett

Yasanne Garrett

I carry my crown

Wherever I go

Sometimes it's not visible,

But it does show

Atop of my head

Is where it should be

Not for you,

But for me to see.

Sometimes I'm discouraged

And have a ways to go

But those who uplift me

Will make sure I'm whole.

I went a different path

The one less traveled

It may seem that I'm put together

But at home I'm unraveled

I cry in my room

And pray for relief

The ache is unbearable

The secrets I keep.

It's okay to stumble

Parallel Lives

Yasanne Garrett

I've been where you been

I've done what you've done

I've thought how you thought

I've became what you become

I haven't acted out

Or gotten even with the one

Who raped my soul

And made my heart numb.

Cerebral parts

Entangled in matter

Reoccurring dreams

Of being battered.

I mean bitter

Cause it brews each day

My insides engulfed

With unbelievable rage.

Fighting myself

The other me

Trying to reclaim

My victory

Belt from the predecessor

Who took it away

The Storm Is Over Now

Pure thoughts of love

Were now on delay.

No arrival certain

Consciousness intact

Hold your Sister's hand

Help her get her life back!

Yasanne Garrett

Yasanne Garrett

The tears I carry
Are mostly from pain
The anxiety to restart
My life over again.

From marriage, kids, divorce
No help no relief
I forgot about HER
The most important part of me.

The HER that had dreams
A vision a joy
Diplomas, careers,
Promotions, employs.

Milk for nursing
Sleepless nights
Hair disheveled
No left, no right.

But this is HER
And SHE is ME
I'm more than this shell
I'm intrinsic and free.

Unearthed the calm
Quiet and still
No more I should've
Now it's I WILL!

The Storm Is Over Now

I will think bigger
I will walk taller
I will love deeper
I will not falter.

For if I fall
It won't hurt at all
Cause my Sisters will be there
To catch my fall.

Yasanne Garrett

I'M IN THE EQUATION

Yasanne Garrett

Life engulfs the best of us
into a realm in which we
reach for constant craving of friendships
that have diminished to
audible sounds of whines and cries.

We latch onto who latches on to us
sucking the life away from each breast,
no longer having the
kinship of conversation of our
once closest female friends.

She walks with confidence in her
Blazer and heels.
She looks put together with her
heavy makeup and dangling
earrings.

I used to be her
with a sense of magnetic north,
but seemingly distant from the
midpoint of woman meets
motherhood.

To be her and laugh with like tongues
of business and independence.
To be her to discover who she is
underneath the smelly
oversized shirt, swollen breasts, and greasy hair.

Womb engorged from the force of
permeable lives.
Maternal instincts heightened at the
sound of cries

I drop everything
to soothe
My sons, my daughters, my community
until they are full from nourishment
'til the next feeding.

The Storm Is Over Now

Yasanne Garrett

The circumstances that brought me
to this time and place
is what made me, not break me.

I am still here,
but they don't know why I
am here.

I wanted to leave, but
the battle of the halves were
emerging.
Caring but not wanting to.
Smiling, but
hating.
calm, but
chaotic.

I managed
to divide myself into
pieces of perfection of pie.
Those tasting the bit that I have
left,
left me malnourished on crumbs of
nothing.

They hear the constant growls of
hunger.
They see the heaviness of
anguish, and yet they still
disrupt my energy.

The Storm Is Over Now

They see me go without and
manage.
They despise me and
whisper "how did she
manage"?

Whatever they think I am,
they know I am mysteriously made.

Decreasing while YOU increase
magnification.
Writing as they chip off
The creative brain by
bouncing questions, scenarios, and
freebies.

Let them think
Let them wonder
Let them doubt.

I am here, and
I am proof
that YOU live!

Yasanne Garrett

Who Are You?

Yasanne Garrett

I am rich
filled with the abundance of
blessings and favor.

I am poor
lacking funds for material gains.

I am weak
from the things I carry for others.

I am hurt
by the actions of a few men.

I am anxious
to start life over again.

I am tired
of living somebody else's lie.

I am overwhelmed
by the weight of the day.

I am scared
that I just might prevail.

I am loved
by my children.

I am needed
by my family.

The Storm Is Over Now

I am powerful,
because I am in tune to the cries of others.

I am just like you-
searching for a word in the darkness
to help me live another day.
To help me stay afloat.
To not fall in front of my kids.

Who am I?
I am a Woman!
and in due time,
I will be healed!

Yasanne Garrett

Yasanne Garrett

I woke up unchained to the prompt of
thoughts.
I can maneuver the room and
not just pivot on one foot.
What was beyond the
room shook my core.
The knob aged and metallic.
The walls lilac and
flowery.
The floor creaking from
ignored upkeep,
And here I am
between door, windows, and walls.

Did they unhinge me
in the middle of the night?

Did they forget to lock the chain?
The bed seems closer,
or
Did I move?

Years of imprisonment
abducted from my
world, my beliefs, my thoughts.

Not realizing that all I had to do
was turn the knob,
go downstairs, walk out the
front door, and
start my own
conversation.

The Storm Is Over Now

Biography

Yasanne J. Garrett is a graduate of Lebanon Community High School in Lebanon, IL. Ms. Garrett graduated with a BA in English Literature and Writing from McKendree University. While at McKendree, she was inducted into the Sigma Tau Delta English Honor Society. Ms. Garrett wrote articles for The McKendrean and submitted writings for The Montage. Ms. Garrett is active in her community through the Rotary Club, Lebanon Woman's Club, Summer Food Program, and AmeriCorps. She teaches at RTI at an elementary school in District 118. Ms. Garrett has three children: Curtis Jr, Michael, and Trinity. She currently resides in Lebanon, IL. In her spare time, she enjoys reading, writing, the outdoors, serving people, being with friends, watching movies, and traveling.

Yasanne Garrett

Made in the USA
Monee, IL
23 September 2020

43221749R10036